CURIOUS
QUESTIONS &
ANSWERS about...

Saving
the Earth

> Would you rather go rowing on a river or diving in the ocean?

> If you could be any animal for a day, which would you choose?

> Are you good at recycling?

> Do you prefer running or cycling?

> Are you as wild as wind power or as sunny as solar?

> What habitat does your favourite animal live in?

Words by Camilla de la Bédoyère

Illustrations by Richard Watson

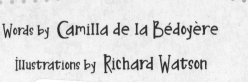

Why is our planet in peril?

Our beautiful planet is in peril because we haven't been taking good care of it. Earth is a precious home for all of us, and the plants and animals that live here too.

How many people are on the planet?

There are more than 7.7 billion people. That's 7,700,000,000 humans! Every one of us has an important job to do. Let's work together to save the Earth!

What is air?

The air is made up of gases and it's wrapped around Earth like a snug blanket. It's called the atmosphere.

21% oxygen

78% nitrogen

1% other gases, including carbon dioxide

Humans breathe in oxygen and breathe out carbon dioxide.

A gas called nitrogen makes up most of the atmosphere. Which gas makes up the next biggest part of the atmosphere?

Plants' leaves take in carbon dioxide to make food. They give out oxygen.

Why does Earth need a blanket?

A blanket of air keeps our planet the perfect temperature!

1. As the Sun's energy reaches Earth's atmosphere, some of it travels through and warms the surface

2. Earth's surface releases heat and some of it escapes back into space

3. Gases in the atmosphere trap some of the heat and reflect it back to Earth, keeping our planet a lovely warm place to live. This is called the greenhouse effect

Atmosphere

The gases in the atmosphere that trap the heat, such as carbon dioxide and methane, are called greenhouse gases.

The world's oceans are warming up and melting my icy Arctic home.

Is Earth getting hotter?

Yes! Things humans do are creating more greenhouse gases. This means that more heat is trapped, so Earth is getting too warm. This is called global warming. Our weather is being affected – we call that climate change.

Did you know?

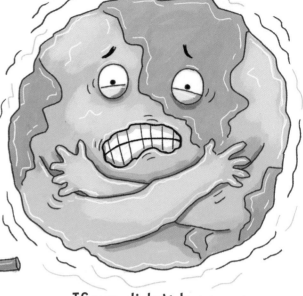

Carbon dioxide

Plants are great at mopping up extra **carbon dioxide** and pumping lots of **oxygen** into the air! That's why we need forests, fields and parks.

Oxygen

If we didn't have an **atmosphere** there would be no air to breathe, and Earth's average temperature would be a very chilly −6°C!

There are more than one billion **cows** in the world, and almost all of them are kept on farms. They all make greenhouse gases when they fart and burp.

Sometimes Earth is called the **Goldilocks planet** because its distance from the Sun means it's just the right temperature for us.

Too hot!

Just right!

Too cold!

5000 TODAY!

You can plant a **tree** to help keep Earth's atmosphere healthy. Some trees are more than 5000 years old.

Scientists looked at how hot the Earth was in the last 100 years and found the five **hottest** years have been since 2010.

Plants make perfect **presents** for people who care about the planet!

Trees can be used to make all of these things: soap, shampoo, rubber gloves, chocolate, paper, clothes and medicines. When trees are cut down, it's important that new ones are planted.

If you lined up all the **cars** in the world they could stretch round it 40 times! Think of all the dirty gases they are putting in the air, and leave your car at home whenever you can!

Trains are a greener way to travel than planes because they make up to six times less dirty gas.

We are taking too many **fish** from the sea. Some fishing nets are more than 60 metres wide and can trap tens of thousands of fish at a time.

What is dirty energy?

Burning oil, gas, wood and coal gives us energy to power our homes and vehicles. This puts more greenhouse gases in the air, and causes pollution.

Pollution is something in the environment that is harmful or poisonous.

Oil, gas and coal are called fossil fuels because they formed inside Earth long ago, from dead animals and plants!

Smoke containing harmful gases

This power station is burning coal. Most air pollution comes from burning fossil fuels

How can bikes help us save the planet?

Cycling, skate-boarding and walking are clean, green ways to get around. You can travel one kilometre by bike in about three minutes, by skateboard in about six minutes, or on foot in about 10 minutes.

This cycle lane is made up of solar panels. They use the Sun's energy to make electricity for lots of people.

Solar panels

What is clean energy?

Not all power comes from dirty fossil fuels. The great news is that there are loads of ways of making clean, green energy!

Wind turbines can turn wind energy into electricity, or other types of power

The energy of flowing water can be used to make hydroelectric power

Wind power

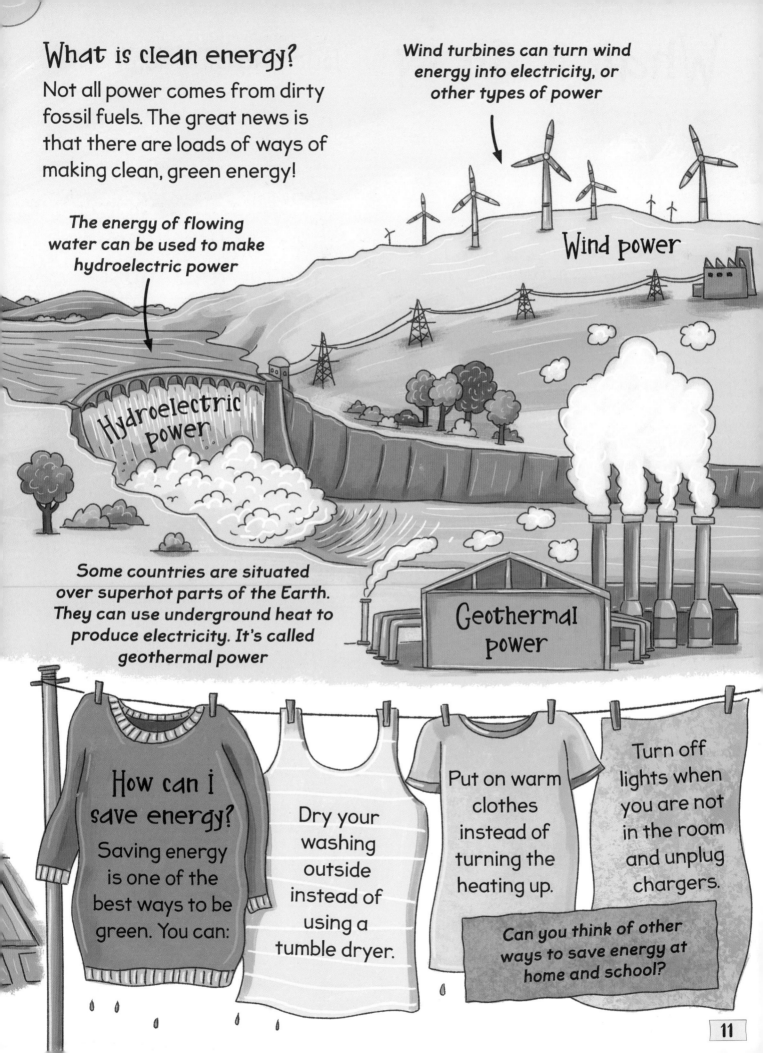

Hydroelectric power

Some countries are situated over superhot parts of the Earth. They can use underground heat to produce electricity. It's called geothermal power

Geothermal power

How can I save energy?

Saving energy is one of the best ways to be green. You can:

Dry your washing outside instead of using a tumble dryer.

Put on warm clothes instead of turning the heating up.

Turn off lights when you are not in the room and unplug chargers.

Can you think of other ways to save energy at home and school?

Why are jellyfish blooming?

Jellyfish love warm water, and as the world's oceans get warmer, the number of jellyfish is rising. Large numbers can even form massive groups, or blooms. The fish aren't so happy, as jellyfish eat them!

Seals that normally eat the fish now have less food. The damage we do to our planet affects all living things.

Why did my colourful home turn white?

Coral reefs need clean, warm water to survive. When the water gets too hot, or dirty, the coral animals die, and the reef turns white.

Why are the oceans dirty?

Our oceans are dirtier than ever because lots of plastic waste has been dumped in the water. Plastic in the ocean gets broken down into tiny pieces, and animals eat them.

How can I help turtles?

Some turtles try to eat plastic bags floating in the sea. They think the bags are their favourite food – jellyfish – and the plastic kills them.

Join a seaside clean-up to help keep beaches clean.

Always take your rubbish home and recycle as much of it as you can.

Ask for paper straws instead of plastic ones, which often end up in the sea.

You can help us turtles and other sea creatures by using canvas or long-life shopping bags instead of plastic ones.

When you go on holiday, don't buy souvenirs that are made from animals or their homes.

How many?

More than **80** countries already use wind power to produce electricity.

In Japan, people use wooden chopsticks to eat. Every year, they get through **90,000** tonnes of them! Can you think of some fun ways to reuse chopsticks?

There is so much heat deep inside Earth that it could provide us with enough power for **1,000,000** years!

1
The number of drinks cans you need to recycle to save energy for **4** hours of TV.

Make sure all your light bulbs are the new energy-saving ones. They last up to **15** times longer and can be recycled!

640
The number of litres of water a garden sprinkler uses in an hour. Use a watering can instead!

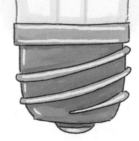

85% of the world's energy still comes from fossil fuels, although many people are working hard to reduce this. Are you?

100 The number of trees you could save from being cut down if your whole class recycle paper for a year.

It takes **50** times as much energy to make a battery as there is stored in the battery! Use rechargeable batteries whenever you can.

The Great Pacific Garbage Patch, a mass of litter floating in the North Pacific Ocean, covers around **1.6 million** square kilometres.

Pacific Ocean

10 The number of litres of clean water in a toilet flush.

Only **3%** of the water on Earth is fresh (not salty), and most of that is frozen. This is why we need to save water where we can.

Where does wee go?

All of the waste water from our homes gets carried away in underground pipes. They're called sewers.

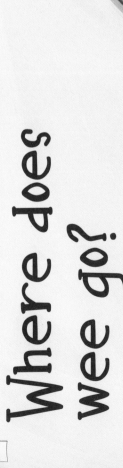

Why are showers best?

A bath uses about 80 litres of water, but a shower uses about 40 litres instead.

Cleaning water uses lots of energy. Turn off the tap while you are brushing your teeth. Can you think of other ways to save water?

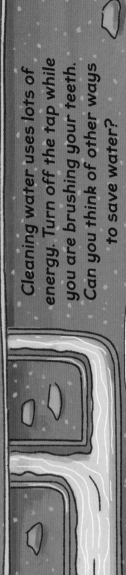

That stinks!

Sewers carry the waste water to a place where it is cleaned so it can be used again

Some sewers also collect rainwater. If the sewer overflows, it empties into rivers or the ocean!

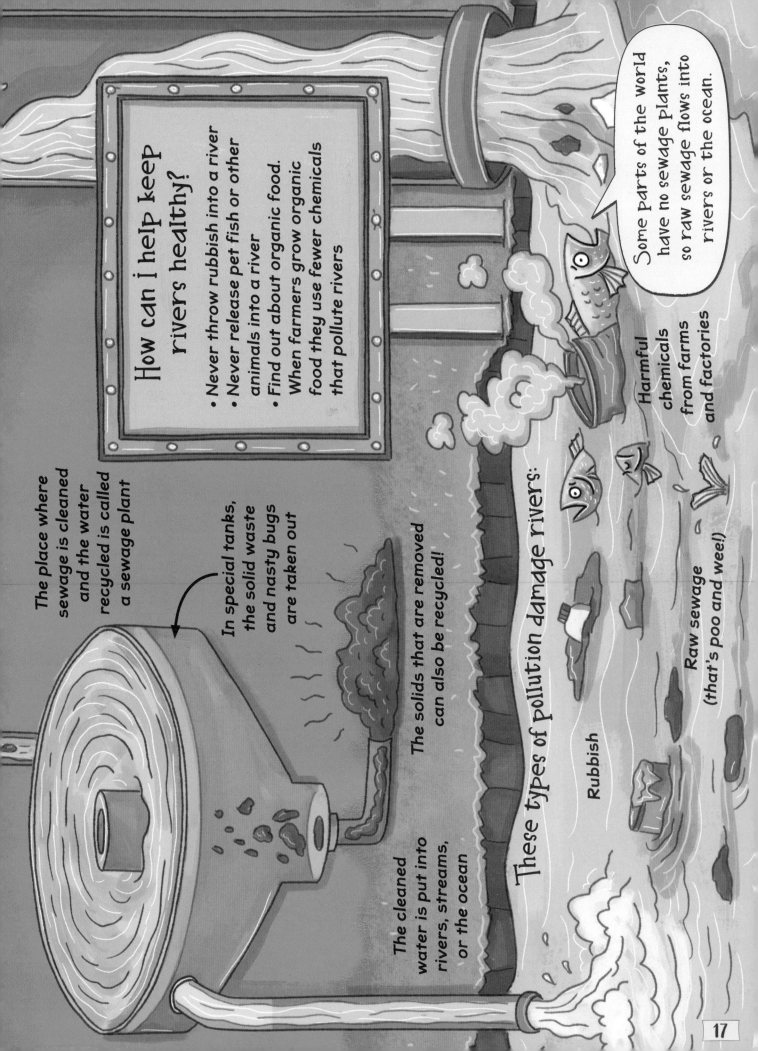

How far did my banana travel?

The distance food travels from where it was grown, to where it will be eaten, is measured in food miles.

1 This banana travelled by truck to get to a boat

50 miles

2 Then it crossed an ocean

5000 miles

3 Then it was put on a lorry and taken to a supermarket

70 miles

4 We bought it and it travelled in our car to get to our home

5 miles

5 It came with me on my bike to school

2 miles

How many food miles does this banana have? Which part of its journey used the least energy?

How can food waste be turned into energy?

When food rots it gives off methane. This can be collected and used for cooking, or heating homes. Plant waste can also be used to make fuel for cars.

4 The methane is used to power electricity generators

5 Electricity is supplied to homes

3 Bacteria in the tank eat the waste, which gives off methane as it breaks down

Methane can also be collected from my poo!

1 Food waste is collected from homes, supermarkets and restaurants

2 All the waste goes in a special sealed tank, where no oxygen can reach it

Who has green fingers?

I do! I grow fruit and veg in my garden so these foods have no food miles!

I put the compost on my garden to help new plants grow. Thanks worms!

Why are worms really useful?

We munch up leftover food, peelings, eggshells and garden waste. We turn it into compost.

19

Would you rather?

Would you rather save water by sharing a **bath** with your dog, or by giving yourself a time limit on your **showers**?

You want to recycle your old toys. Would you rather take them to a **charity shop**, or **swap** them with a friend?

If you get cold, would you rather warm up by **running** on the spot or by wearing a big **jumper**?

Would you rather be a wriggly worm eating **rotten food** in a compost heap, or a dung beetle munching on **elephant poo**?

Would you rather try to make a **space rocket** from cans, or a **submarine** from a plastic bottle?

If you worked in a safari park, would you rather **teach** people about nature... or **check** a crocodile's teeth?

You want to cut down your food miles. Would you rather catch your own **fish**, keep your own **hens**, or grow your own **tomatoes**?

Which environment would you most like to work to protect – the **Amazon rainforest** or the chilly **North Pole**?

21

What is an animal's home called?

The place where an animal lives is called a habitat. Forests, grasslands, rivers and deserts are types of habitat. When habitats are destroyed, some animals lose their homes, and might go extinct.

Bornean orang-utan

Where did your home go?

In Borneo, diverse forests the size of 180 football pitches are cut down every hour so palm trees can be grown. Avoid buying foods made with palm oil and you can help us keep our homes.

Bengal tiger

How can you help to save animal habitats?

Wildlife charities work to save habitats, and raising money for them is a good way to help. It's also a good idea to only buy food and products that have been made without harming wild habitats.

I'm doing a sponsored silence to raise money to protect wild habitats.

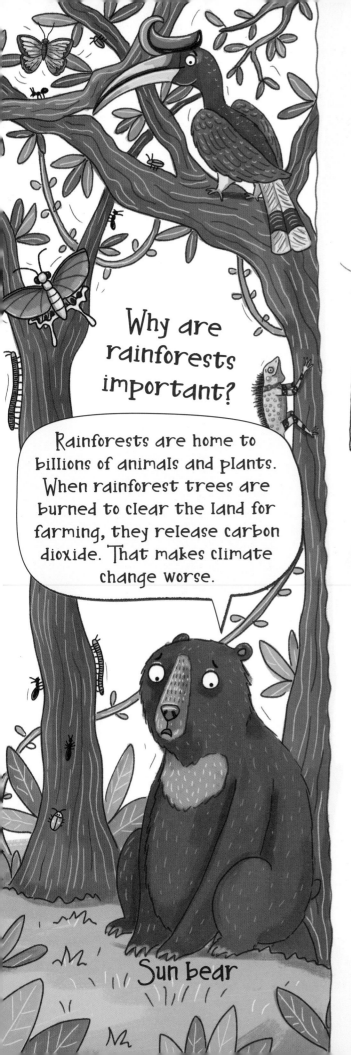

Why are rainforests important?

Rainforests are home to billions of animals and plants. When rainforest trees are burned to clear the land for farming, they release carbon dioxide. That makes climate change worse.

Sun bear

What causes extinction?

Extinction is when a type of animal or plant dies out so there are none left on Earth. There are lots of reasons for extinction, but today humans are doing so much damage to the world that we are putting many animals at risk.

Going...
Beluga sturgeons are under threat because they are fished for their valuable eggs

Going...
Rhinos are hunted and killed because some people want their horns

Gone
Golden toads probably went extinct because of global warming

Where does all the rubbish go?

When we throw rubbish away we sort it into different bins. Some of it will end up in landfill or being burned, which is very bad for the environment. It's better to go zero! That means trying to create no rubbish at all.

Painted turtles

Some of this rubbish will never rot. It will stay in the ground for hundreds, or even thousands of years.

What's that stink?

A landfill is a huge hole in the ground where rubbish is put. As the rubbish rots, it gives off methane. It's a more harmful greenhouse gas than carbon dioxide.

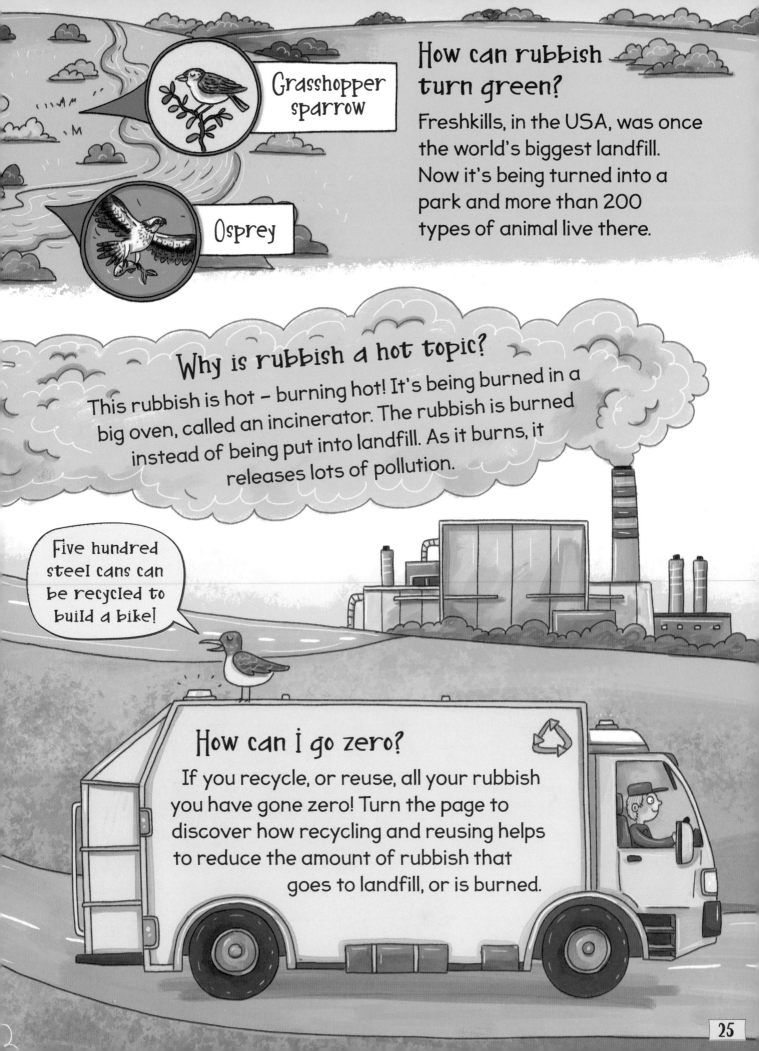

Grasshopper sparrow

Osprey

How can rubbish turn green?

Freshkills, in the USA, was once the world's biggest landfill. Now it's being turned into a park and more than 200 types of animal live there.

Why is rubbish a hot topic?

This rubbish is hot – burning hot! It's being burned in a big oven, called an incinerator. The rubbish is burned instead of being put into landfill. As it burns, it releases lots of pollution.

Five hundred steel cans can be recycled to build a bike!

How can I go zero?

If you recycle, or reuse, all your rubbish you have gone zero! Turn the page to discover how recycling and reusing helps to reduce the amount of rubbish that goes to landfill, or is burned.

What are the three Rs?

Reduce, Reuse and Recycle! By cutting down the amount of energy we use and waste we create, we can help to make Earth a better place.

REDUCE

Cutting down the amount of meat you eat can cut greenhouse gases.

REUSE

Using paper more than once means fewer trees will be cut down – and save a forest.

RECYCLE

You can save energy by recycling. That helps protect Earth's atmosphere from damage.

Can poo be recycled?

Yes it can!

Elephant, rhino and kangaroo poo can be used to make paper

Llama poo can be burned on fires to keep people warm, or cook their food

The solid sludge that is collected at sewage farms can be turned into fertiliser. Farmers put it on their fields to help plants grow

How can we create less rubbish?

Plastic can be difficult to recycle, so try not to buy things that come in lots of plastic packaging.

Use a reusable water bottle and fill it with tap water.

Carry your lunch in reusable tubs or beeswax wrappers instead of plastic wrap.

Use a toothbrush made from bamboo, not plastic.

What are we doing to save the planet?

All over the world, people are working hard to save the planet for your future – at home, on farms and in the workplace. Saving the planet is a job for everyone.

What is conservation?
Conservation is the work people do to protect wild and special places.

My job is to look after the Great Barrier Reef and teach people about the animals that live here.

We collect wood to burn at home, for cooking and heating, but we are planting new trees to replace the wood we use.

What's a solar farm?

A solar farm is a place with lots of solar panels. The panels collect sunlight and turn it into electricity.

The largest solar farms are in hot countries. They have more than 2 million solar panels.

I'm a solar-powered cleaning machine! At this solar farm in India, we keep the panels clear of sand so they can keep soaking up the sunlight.

I live in the Amazon rainforest. I take care of this precious habitat so it will still be here for my children and grandchildren.

I'm in Antarctica, counting penguins to see how healthy this colony is.

We can all do our part to help save the Earth!

A compendium of questions

How can I feed wild birds?

You can grow flowers that will make seeds for the birds to eat in winter. You can also buy bird food and hang it from trees in bird feeders.

It's a good idea to fill up a bird bath, or leave a bowl of water out so birds can drink and wash — far from any place where cats can hide!

How can I use less plastic?

Think about whether you need to buy a product in plastic. Liquid soap, for example, comes in plastic bottles, but a bar of soap is wrapped in paper.

What can I do for nature on a day out?

Enjoy looking at plants and animals, but avoid picking flowers or disturbing animal homes. Always take your rubbish home.

What should I do with old clothes?

Clothes can be recycled, they can be cut up and used as rags for cleaning, or if they are in good condition you can sell or swap them, or take them to charity shops.